Spiritual Living in a Secular World

DISCOVERY SERIES BIBLE STUDY
For individuals or groups

Every generation needs to see the timelessness of the Bible. Even a story like Daniel in the lions' den can become food for thought throughout the rest of our lives.

The Bible isn't just about telling us what we should do. It's far more enlightening than that. Each chapter tells us enough about God and ourselves to show us how to line up with what He is doing in our world.

This is the conviction of Bill Crowder of the RBC Ministries staff. In the following pages, he helps us to see that what God reveals about himself in the unfolding drama of Daniel can put us in touch with the great timeless purposes of life.

—*Mart DeHaan*
RBC Ministries

This Discovery Series Bible Study is based on
Spiritual Living in a Secular Culture (QO724), one of the popular Discovery Series
booklets from RBC Ministries. Find out more about Discovery Series at
www.discoveryseries.org

Discovery House Publishers is affiliated with RBC Ministries,
Grand Rapids, Michigan.

Requests for permission to quote from this book should be directed to:
Permissions Department, Discovery House Publishers, PO Box 3566, Grand Rapids, MI 49501,
or contact us by e-mail at permissionsdept@dhp.org

DISCOVERY HOUSE
P U B L I S H E R S®

Managing Editor: Dave Branon
Study Guide questions: Dave Branon
Graphic Design: Steve Gier

COVER PHOTO:
Composite images from Stock.Xchng

INSIDE PHOTOS:
Via Stock.Xchng: pp. 6, 10, 18, 21, 30, 38, 41. *Via RGB Stock:* Michal Zacharzewski, p.8; L Goh, p.11;
Sanja Gjenero, pp.20 and 54; Adrian van Leen, p.48; Krzysztof Szkurlatowski / 12frames.eu, p.50; Mirna Sentic, p.51.
Via Freerange Stock: Jo-Anne Brandes, p.28. *Via Stockvault:* François Huynh, p.31. *Via Wikipedia Commons:* Rolf Müller, p.56.
Via Public Domain: Benjamin West, p.40

ISBN: 978-1-57293-808-3
Printed in the United States of America
First Printing in 2013

Table of Contents

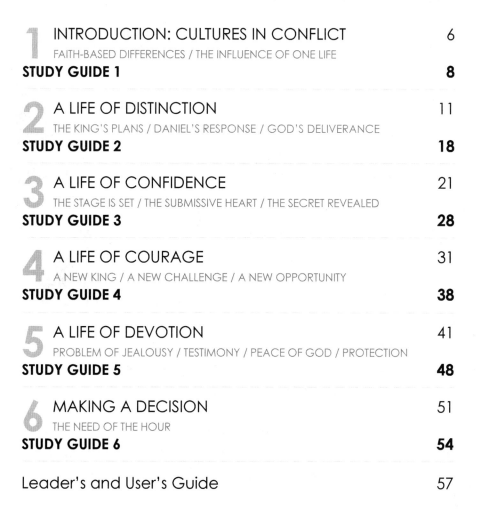

How To Use
DISCOVERY SERIES BIBLE STUDIES

The Purpose

The Discovery Series Bible Study (DSBS) series provides assistance to pastors and lay leaders in guiding and teaching fellow Christians with lessons adapted from RBC Ministries Discovery Series booklets and supplemented from items taken from the pages of *Our Daily Bread.* The DSBS series uses the inductive study method to help Christians understand the Bible more clearly.

The Format

READ: Each DSBS book is divided into a series of lessons. For each lesson, you will read a few pages that will give you insight into one aspect of the overall study. Included in some studies will be FOCAL POINT and TIME OUT FOR THEOLOGY segments to help you think through the material. These can be used as discussion starters for group sessions.

RESPOND: At the end of the reading is a two-page STUDY GUIDE to help participants respond to and reflect on the subject. If you are the leader of a group study, ask each member to preview the STUDY GUIDE before the group gets together. Don't feel that you have to work your way through each question in the STUDY GUIDE; let the interest level of the participants dictate the flow of the discussion. The questions are designed for either group or individual study. Here are the parts of that guide:

MEMORY VERSE: A short Scripture passage that focuses your thinking on the biblical truth at hand and can be used for memorization. You might suggest memorization as a part of each meeting.

WARMING UP: A general interest question that can foster discussion (group) or contemplation (individual).

THINKING THROUGH: Questions that will help a group or a student interact with the reading. These questions help drive home the critical concepts of the book.

DIGGING IN: An inductive study of a related passage of Scripture, reminding the group or the student of the importance of Scripture as the final authority.

GOING FURTHER: A two-part wrap-up of the response: REFER suggests ways to compare the ideas of the lesson with teachings in other parts of the Bible. REFLECT challenges the group or the learner to apply the teaching in real life.

OUR DAILY BREAD: After each STUDY GUIDE session will be an *Our Daily Bread* article that relates to the topic. You can use this for further reflection or for an introduction to a time of prayer.

Go to the Leader's and User's Guide on page 57 for further suggestions about using this Discovery Series Bible Study.

1 INTRODUCTION

Cultures in Conflict

n the 1960s, American citizens were fighting battles on a number of fronts. In Vietnam, our soldiers were dying in an unpopular war. At home, we were engaged in a series of conflicts, each of which wrote new chapters of American history. The news headlines screamed out that the culture of the United States was being challenged and segmented as never before. Here are some examples:

- **Generational conflict,** with young people challenging the authority, institutions, and hard-earned wealth that their parents' generation was bequeathing to them.

- **Racial conflict,** with an emerging African-American community that was finally standing up to claim the equal rights granted to these citizens by their national constitution.

- **Religious conflict,** with the historic traditions of mainstream churches being challenged by an enthusiastic youth-based movement calling itself the Jesus People.

The social upheaval of the 1960s foreshadowed a series of social conflicts that would seriously threaten the unity of the nation. The "Culture Wars," as they became known, divided society over a series of moral issues often linked to religious convictions.

 Impact of Faith-based Differences

The role of personal faith in a divided culture is unavoidable. As Os Guinness wrote in his book *The Call:* "In today's world, differences can be seen to make a difference. Beliefs have consequences" (p. 59).

What begin as theoretically different views of God, the world, justice, humanness, and freedom end in radically divergent ways of living and dying.

In the past, some people of faith have withdrawn from society into insulated communities separated from the cultural fray. Others have organized themselves into political action groups. Still others have found themselves destined to show that, in the hand of God, one life can make a difference—even without the guarantee of civil rights and even in the middle of a foreign culture.

 The Influence of One Life

About six hundred years before the birth of Christ, Daniel saw his nation overrun and his life uprooted. Together with a group of other Jewish hostages, he was led as a captive to a place called Babylon—a foreign culture hundreds of miles and light-years away from the relative stability of Jerusalem. In a region now called Iraq, Daniel experienced the challenge of living out his faith in a culture devoted to a vastly different set of values and priorities.

As Daniel and his friends entered this new world, they would live out convictions that were destined to put them out of step with their powerful captors. Yet, in the middle of a pagan world, Daniel became

- a governmental leader, serving in appointed positions under three kings;
- a historian, recording what God did in his day; and
- a prophet, engaged in predicting the future and speaking truth to leaders.

In the unfolding drama of the Bible, Daniel is a case-study of personal faith in a hostile culture.

Cultures in Conflict

1

STUDY GUIDE
read pages 6–7

MEMORY VERSE
John 17:15—
"I do not pray that You should take them out of the world, but that You should keep them from the evil one."

To understand how cultural differences affect both secular and spiritual lives—and how one person can make a difference.

Warming Up

Can you name someone you think is doing well at living in a world of cultural challenges yet remaining true to God in the conflict? What trait of this person would you like to emulate?

Thinking Through

1. What societal conflicts do you feel are most relevant and most challenging in the community where you live?

2. In what way do you see religious conflicts affecting your world? What is the best way to address such faith-based differences?

3. As you begin to think about the Daniel story, discuss with others what you admire most about Daniel and the way he lived in a hostile, secular culture.

Going Further

Refer

1. Examine 1 John 2:15 and discuss what it means in real life: "Do not love the world or the things in the world. If anyone loves the world, the love of the Father is not in him."

1. What does it mean that the people to whom Jesus refers "are not of the world" (v. 14)?

2. Jesus' solution to the problem of cultural conflict is not to remove Christians. What does He suggest will help them the most (v. 15)?

3. What document will help those who are in the world not to be defeated (v. 17)?

12 While I was with them in the world, I kept them in Your name. Those whom You gave Me I have kept; and none of them is lost except the son of perdition, that the Scripture might be fulfilled. 13 But now I come to You, and these things I speak in the world, that they may have My joy fulfilled in themselves. 14 I have given them Your word; and the world has hated them because they are not of the world, just as I am not of the world. 15 I do not pray that You should take them out of the world, but that You should keep them from the evil one. 16 They are not of the world, just as I am not of the world. 17 Sanctify them by Your truth. Your word is truth.

Prayer Time ▶

Use the *Our Daily Bread* article on the next page as a guide for a devotional and meditation time relating to the culture.

Reflect

1. When you look around at the way today's culture conflicts with Christianity, what do you see as the top conflict that has to be dealt with by believers?

2. In what ways do you see Daniel's story holding out a promise of hope for you as you consider today's cultural conflicts?

The Spirit of the Age

Every age has its own thoughts, ideas, and values that influence the culture, the "spirit of the age." It is the kind of growing consensus that morally lulls us to sleep, gradually causing us to accept society's latest values.

The apostle Paul called this corrupting atmosphere the "course of this world." Describing the lives of the believers at Ephesus before they encountered Christ, he said that they were "dead in trespasses and sins" and "walked according to the course of this world" (Ephesians 2:1–2). This is the world's peer pressure—a satanically inspired system of values and ideas that cultivates a lifestyle that is independent of God.

Jesus intends for us to live in the world (John 17:15), so worldly influence is nearly impossible to escape. But He has given us His Word to so permeate our thinking that we don't have to become conformed to the world's values (Romans 12:1–2). Instead, God helps us walk in His light (Ephesians 5:8), in the Spirit (Galatians 5:25), in love (Ephesians 5:2), in truth (3 John 4), and in Christ (Colossians 2:6).

As we walk in God's power and spend time in His Word, He gives us the strength to live according to kingdom values and not the spirit of the age.

—*Dennis Fisher*

EPHESIANS 2:1–2—

You He made alive, who were dead in trespasses and sins, in which you once walked according to the course of this world.

■ Read today's *Our Daily Bread* at **www.rbc.org/odb**

2

A Life of Distinction

DANIEL 1

As Daniel's story opens, Judah is being invaded and business as usual has stopped. The prophet Jeremiah knew why. For more than twenty years he had pleaded with the citizens of Judah to return to their God. He warned them that if they refused, they would be captured by the Babylonians and taken captive for seventy years (Jeremiah 25:1–11). Because Judah had turned a deaf ear, Daniel now writes as a witness to the invasion and describes what happened in its wake.

The King's Plans
(1:1–7)

In the third year of the reign of Jehoiakim king of Judah, Nebuchadnezzar king of Babylon came to Jerusalem and besieged it. And the Lord gave Jehoiakim king of Judah into his hand, with some of the articles of the house of God, which he carried into the land of Shinar to the house of his god; and he brought the articles into the treasure house of his god (vv. 1–2).

King Nebuchadnezzar of Babylon decided to take the best and brightest of the captive nation of Judah and use them to advance his nation. Unlike Ahasuerus in the book of Esther, who took women captive for his own personal pleasure, Nebuchadnezzar chose the finest young men to better the nation.

Then the king instructed Ashpenaz, the master of his eunuchs, to bring some of the children of Israel and some of the king's descendants and some of the nobles, young men . . . (vv. 3–4).

■ FOCAL POINT

"What kind of character did Nebuchadnezzar have? Later in his reign, he demonstrates his absolute cruelty in killing the sons of Judah's king before their father's eyes. . . . Nebuchadnezzar had another man roasted slowly to death over a fire. This king was an expert in torture; his cruel imagination fueled his evil deeds. And Nebuchadnezzar's word was absolute law. So these young teenagers faced this moral test knowing that they had to either comply with the king's demands or risk an unimaginably horrible death."

—Ray Stedman
Adventuring Through the Bible

■ FOCAL POINT

"Jeremiah's denunciations of the Jerusalem populace imply that not many godly homes existed at this time; but surely some did, to account for fine young men like these. Coming from such homes, and with the type of personality demonstrated in the story, each of the four would have found captive conditions difficult."

— Leon Wood
A Commentary on Daniel

He pooled the best minds and abilities to make Babylon stronger. This selection process demanded that they meet high standards. Notice that he chose:

. . . young men in whom there was no blemish, but good-looking, gifted in all wisdom, possessing knowledge and quick to understand, who had ability to serve in the king's palace (v. 4).

That's an impressive list. They had to be good-looking and without physical defect, skilled in wisdom and able to learn, and capable in the area of discernment.

These young men were going to be turned into wise men. Notice verses 4–7:

. . . whom they might teach the language and literature of the Chaldeans. And the king appointed for them a daily provision of the king's delicacies and of the wine which he drank, and three years of training for them, so that at the end of that time they might serve before the king. Now from among those of the sons of Judah were Daniel, Hananiah, Mishael, and Azariah. To them the chief of the eunuchs gave names: he gave Daniel the name Belteshazzar; to Hananiah, Shadrach; to Mishael, Meshach; and to Azariah, Abed-Nego.

This strategy presented some subtle challenges. Yes, they would be better off than the slaves of Babylon, but their situation produced challenges others would not face. They came in several forms:

ENVIRONMENT: These are the problems that either shape our character or reveal it. The key here is that having been taken to a strange, pagan land at an impressionable age, Daniel will maintain his purity.

LIFESTYLE: "The king's delicacies" were not necessarily bad dietarily. It was food that had been offered and dedicated to Babylon's false gods. To eat that food was to endorse those idols.

ALLEGIANCE. The king's plan was a subtle attack on the young men's center of gravity. First, he sought to change their thinking by requiring that they study under the astrologers of Babylon. The second goal was to change their worship by changing their names. They all had names that pointed to the God of Israel: (Daniel, "God is my judge"; Hananiah, "God is gracious"; Mishael, "who is like God?"; Azariah, "helped by God"). The name changes were to indicate a shift in allegiance to the Babylonian gods.

What was Nebuchadnezzar's goal? By changing their way of thinking,

◼ FOCAL POINT

"As a young boy, Daniel lived during the reign of King Josiah of Judah, that vigorous reformer who attempted to undo 57 shameless years of apostasy under his father and grandfather. The temple was repaired, and the Book of the Law was found and read to the king and the people. As a result, a national revival swept the land. Tragically, this revival had no effect on the sons of Josiah, and when they succeeded to the throne they only sought to undo the righteous works of their father. There is every reason to believe, however, that the revival of Josiah's time had a deep and lasting effect upon a young boy named Daniel, who determined to be faithful to God in all his life."

—Donald K. Campbell
Daniel: God's Man in a Secular Society

eating, and worshiping, he hoped to change their way of living. How would they respond to this character test?

Daniel's Response
(1:8–14)

But Daniel purposed in his heart that he would not defile himself with the portion of the king's delicacies, nor with the wine which he drank; therefore he requested of the chief of the eunuchs that he might not defile himself (v. 8).

Daniel recognized that eating the king's food raised an issue of principle. He saw something about the food that prompted a response similar to what we find King David saying in Psalm 119: "Your word I have hidden in my heart, that I might not sin against You" (v. 11).

What did Daniel see? First, the king's food wasn't kosher—not prepared according to the dietary principles of Israel. Life in exile, however, made it impossible for the Jewish young men to keep many of the Torah- and temple-based laws of Israel. But what was probably a greater issue for Daniel was a pattern that shows up in other places in his life. He didn't want to do anything that would honor the gods of Babylon. Eating and drinking food and wine offered to idols was probably what Daniel saw as a violation of the Word and the honor of his God.

The easy route would have been to go with the flow: "When in Babylon, do as the Babylonians do." But Daniel's objective was obedience in spite of his environment.

Daniel and friends took a stand the other captives apparently did not take. Notice that Daniel "purposed in his heart." This is the key attitude. If the priority is purity, you must have a desire to obey God and the commitment to act on that desire. Daniel had a variety of options, but he was determined to be true to God. A life committed to God begins with purpose of heart, and from the very beginning of the three-year training period, he was tested on this issue.

Now God had brought Daniel into the favor and goodwill of the chief of the eunuchs. And the chief of the eunuchs said to Daniel, "I fear my lord the king, who has appointed your food and drink. For why should he see your faces looking worse than the young men who are your age? Then you would endanger my head before the king" (vv. 9–10).

Faced with this dilemma, Daniel used diplomacy and showed a proper conscience. Even here we see the work of God in preparation for this moment. Daniel took his stand—and God gave him favor with the chief of the eunuchs.

Then Daniel said to the steward who had been put in charge of him:

"Please test your servants for ten days, and let them give us vegetables to eat and water to drink. Then let our appearance be examined before you, and the appearance of the young men who eat the portion of the king's delicacies; and as you see fit, so deal with your servants." So he consented with them in this matter, and tested them ten days (vv. 12–14).

Daniel went to the warden and asked for a ten-day trial diet of vegetables. I'm a meat-and-potatoes kind of guy, so this isn't very attractive to me. Ten days of vegetables? Not for me. Beyond that, however, this test required a kind of suspension of the laws of nutrition. How could there be a noticeable difference in only ten days? It was a small test of faith that would prepare Daniel for the greater tests of faith to come.

 # God's Deliverance
(1:15–20)

The test worked and showed that Daniel and his friends knew what Israel forgot—God blesses obedience.

At the end of ten days their features appeared better and fatter in flesh than all the young men who ate the portion of the king's delicacies. Thus the steward took away their portion of delicacies and the wine that they were to drink, and gave them vegetables (vv. 15–16).

Daniel and his friends came out better than the others because God worked on their behalf. As a result, the diet was allowed to continue (though, to me, that would be more of a punishment than a reward). Daniel's life had stayed firm because he was committed to a purity that flows from obedience to the Word, and it gave him a foundation for living in a difficult culture.

> *As for these four young men, God gave them knowledge and skill in all literature and wisdom; and Daniel had understanding in all visions and dreams. Now at the end of the days, when the king had said that they should be brought in, the chief of the eunuchs brought them in before Nebuchadnezzar. Then the king interviewed them, and among them all none was found like Daniel, Hananiah, Mishael, and Azariah; therefore they served before the king (vv. 17–19).*

In verse 20, God's blessing is confirmed as Daniel and his friends were declared to be "ten times better" than all the scholars of Babylon.

At the end of their training, Daniel was probably no more than twenty years old. This means he was only sixteen or seventeen when he and the other young men were initially put to the test. At that young age, Daniel was set apart for service and lived a life of distinction in a powerful pagan government of the ancient world.

2 A Life of Distinction

To begin to see what it takes to maintain godliness in the face of tough circumstances.

MEMORY VERSE
Daniel 1:8—

"Daniel purposed in his heart that he would not defile himself."

Warming Up

Think of some of the ways it is possible today to be swayed toward behavior that is not godly. What examples can you recall from times you've had to make a conscious decision to "not defile" yourself.

Thinking Through

1. Jeremiah 25:5 gives a clear picture of what the problems were leading up to the invasion by Babylon. How could the situation best be summarized?

2. Bill Crowder mentions three forms of the challenges Daniel and his friends faced (p. 14). What were they, and what did Crowder mean by each?

3. According to page 15, what did Daniel find to be the problem with the food being offered?

Going Further

Refer

1. How can we relate the following verses to what Daniel faced—and then relate those verses to our situation: 1 Peter 1:14–16; Ephesians 5:25–27; John 14:15; John 15:14?

1. What characteristics of the young men brought to the king would be valuable goals for today's teens who want to serve the Lord (v. 3)? Should a teen be intimidated by the list—thinking he or she just doesn't measure up?

2. What did Daniel have to know ahead of time in order to respond as he did in verse 8? What does that tell us about him in regard to his training?

3. In what ways does God reward young people today for their faithfulness to Him (v. 17)? What about those of us who are beyond the teen years?

³ The king instructed Ashpenaz, the master of his eunuchs, to bring some of the children of Israel. . . , ⁴ young men in whom there was no blemish, but good-looking, gifted in all wisdom, possessing knowledge and quick to understand, ... ⁵ And the king appointed for them a daily provision of the king's delicacies and of the wine which he drank, . . . ⁶ Now from among those of the sons of Judah were Daniel, Hananiah, Mishael, and Azariah. . . . ⁸ But Daniel purposed in his heart that he would not defile himself with the portion of the king's delicacies, . . . therefore he requested of the chief of the eunuchs that he might not defile himself. . . .
¹⁵ At the end of ten days their features appeared better and fatter in flesh than all the young men who ate the portion of the king's delicacies. . . .
¹⁷ As for these four young men, God gave them knowledge and skill in all literature and wisdom; and Daniel had understanding in all visions and dreams.

Prayer Time ⧐

Use the *Our Daily Bread* article on the next page as a guide for a devotional and meditation time relating to the culture.

Reflect

1. As we look at life in the twenty-first century, what are some of the equivalencies to this story? What are the items we must avoid in order to not defile ourselves?

2. What are three lessons we can learn from these four teenagers?

Gaining Respect

When a professional musician nicknamed "Happy" became a Christian, he quit playing in nightclubs and offered his services to a rescue mission. Some time later, he received a phone call from a club manager who wanted to hire him to do a show that would have brought in a lot of money. But Happy turned down the offer, telling the manager that he would be playing at the mission. Happy later said, "He congratulated me. That surprised me. Here was a man who wanted me to play for him, and he was congratulating me for refusing his offer." The manager respected Happy's decision.

Daniel was a captive in a foreign land, but he did not forget his God-honoring principles. He could not in good conscience eat meat that had been dedicated to a pagan god and had not been slaughtered in accordance with Hebrew laws. He asked for a simple fare of vegetables and water, and the steward risked his life to honor his request. I believe he did this because Daniel's noble conduct had earned his respect.

The world looks with disdain on Christians who do not live what they say they believe. That's why we should remain true to our convictions. Consistency of character is what gains the respect of others.

—*Herb Vander Lugt*

DANIEL 1:8—
Daniel purposed in his heart that he would not defile himself.

■ Read today's *Our Daily Bread* at **www.rbc.org/odb**

3

A Life of Confidence

DANIEL 2

Consider the following situations. What do they all have in common?

- a goalkeeper for a World Cup soccer team in a penalty kick shootout
- a surgeon in the midst of a difficult heart-bypass procedure
- an airline pilot trying to land a jet with one engine shut down

All of these challenging situations demand that an individual perform at the highest level of skill in moments of great pressure and scrutiny. And this is where we find Daniel and his friends as the story continues. They will rise above the pressure with a deep confidence in God.

The Stage Is Set
(2:1–13)

Now in the second year of Nebuchadnezzar's reign, Nebuchadnezzar had dreams; and his spirit was so troubled that his sleep left him (v. 1).

This verse epitomizes Shakespeare's line in *Henry IV:* "Uneasy lies the head that wears a crown." Nebuchadnezzar's sleep was disturbed by dreams. But it was one particular dream that concerned him. As one writer put it, the cares of the day became the cares of the night, and the king awoke in turmoil and summoned his advisors. (Daniel and friends were not called, which implies that they were still in training at the time.) Whom did the king call? Verse 2 tells us: "the magicians, the astrologers, the sorcerers, and the Chaldeans."

The "magicians" were the sacred writers or scholars. "The astrologers" were enchanters and sacred priests. "The sorcerers" were involved in the occult and sold herbs and potions. And "the Chaldeans" were the king's wise men.

Once they were all assembled before the king, a dialogue ensued that would show these alleged wise men just how much trouble they were in. Watch the dialogue unfold in verses 3–9:

> *And the king said to them, "I have had a dream, and my spirit is anxious to know the dream." Then the Chaldeans spoke to the king in Aramaic, "O king, live forever! Tell your servants the dream, and we will give the interpretation." The king answered and said to the Chaldeans, "My decision is firm: if you do not make known the dream to me, and its interpretation, you shall be cut in pieces, and your houses shall be made an ash heap. However, if you tell the dream and its interpretation, you shall receive from me gifts, rewards, and great honor. Therefore, tell me the dream and its interpretation."*
>
> *They answered again and said, "Let the king tell his servants the dream, and we will give its interpretation." The king answered and said, "I know for certain that you would gain time, because you see that my decision is firm: if you do not make known the dream to me, there is only one decree*

for you! For you have agreed to speak lying and corrupt words before me till the time has changed. Therefore tell me the dream, and I shall know that you can give me its interpretation."

Their plea for mercy in verses 10–13 revealed the seriousness of the danger they were in:

The Chaldeans answered the king, and said, "There is not a man on earth who can tell the king's matter; therefore no king, lord, or ruler has ever asked such things of any magician, astrologer, or Chaldean. It is a difficult thing that the king requests, and there is no other who can tell it to the king except the gods, whose dwelling is not with flesh." For this reason the king was angry and very furious, and gave the command to destroy all the wise men of Babylon. So the decree went out, and they began killing wise men; and they sought Daniel and his companions, to kill them.

When the Chaldeans told the king that his request to interpret his dream was unfair because only the gods could do such a thing, they unwittingly set the stage for Daniel's God to do just that!

Once they admitted their inability, Nebuchadnezzar exploded. He was so enraged that he ordered all the wise men—including Daniel and the youths in training—to be executed. As a result, Daniel and his friends were arrested.

The Submissive Heart
(2:14–23)

Arioch, the captain of the guard, was sent out to kill all the wise men of Babylon. But when he approached Daniel, Daniel was able to speak to him "with counsel and wisdom" (v. 14). Daniel asked for an explanation and Arioch told him the entire sad story. Making the most of the opportunity,

Daniel went in and asked the king to give him time, that he might tell the king the interpretation (v. 16).

Essentially, Daniel said, "Give me time, and I guarantee the king an answer." This was a huge promise in the face of the failure of the others.

> *Then Daniel went to his house, and made the decision known to Hananiah, Mishael, and Azariah, his companions, that they might seek mercies from the God of heaven concerning this secret, so that Daniel and his companions might not perish with the rest of the wise men of Babylon (vv. 17–18).*

Daniel shared his heart's burden with his friends, and together they began praying. They began to "seek mercies from the God of heaven." This was a powerful expression of their spiritual confidence. They desired that God in His mercy would intervene and rescue them from the execution that had been planned.

> *Then the secret was revealed to Daniel in a night vision. So Daniel blessed the God of heaven. Daniel answered and said: "Blessed be the name of God forever and ever, for wisdom and might are His. And He changes the times and the seasons; He removes kings and raises up kings; He gives wisdom to the wise and knowledge to those who have understanding. He reveals deep and secret things; He knows what is in the darkness, and light dwells with Him. I thank You and praise You, O God of my fathers; You have given me wisdom and might, and have now made known to me what we asked of You, for You have made known to us the king's demand" (vv. 19–23).*

As they prayed, God unveiled the secret of the king's dream to Daniel. Notice in verse 19 the matter-of-fact statement of this answer to prayer. This was not a big surprise! With the proverbial noose still around Daniel's neck, his first response was not to gain relief or to use his knowledge to his own advantage. Rather, it was to worship. And the focus of that worship was the God of power and provision. What great praise was given:

- "Blessed be the name of God," which is an emblem of His character
- "Wisdom and might are His," not Daniel's

- "He changes the times and the seasons," implying total control over all of life
- "He removes kings and raises up kings," for God is sovereign over the nations
- "He gives wisdom . . . and knowledge," as is promised in James 1:5
- "He reveals deep and secret things," including this dream
- "He knows what is in the darkness, and light dwells with Him"

Daniel gave God all praise for answering his prayer (v. 23). What a marvelous display of worship! Would it have been inappropriate for Daniel to thank God for saving His life? Of course not. But it seems that this miraculous rescue was secondary in Daniel's mind to the wonder of the God who performed it.

Daniel's response should cause all of us to examine our heart to see where our own focus would have been:

- on the Blesser, or on the blessings?
- on the Lord of the work, or on the work?
- on the God who answers prayer, or on the answer?

It's all about focus.

And when we fail to put our confidence in God, it's easy to lose our focus. Our perspectives become blurred, and we see the trees rather than the forest. Yet Daniel's focus stayed clear during a time of life-and-death pressure. His heart was locked in on God, and God enabled him to perform rather than wilt under pressure.

 ## The Secret Revealed
(2:24–30)

Daniel moved ahead in confidence that God would prepare the way.

> *Therefore Daniel went to Arioch, whom the king had appointed to destroy the wise men of Babylon. He went and said thus to him: "Do not destroy the*

wise men of Babylon; take me before the king, and I will tell the king the
interpretation." Then Arioch quickly brought Daniel before the king, and
said thus to him, "I have found a man of the captives of Judah, who will
make known to the king the interpretation" (vv. 24–25).

Daniel went to Arioch, who announced to the king that the answer had
been found. When Daniel stood before the king (apparently for the first time,
and still in his teens), the king asked a compelling question:

Are you able to make known to me the dream which I have seen, and its
interpretation? (v. 26).

In other words, was Daniel able to succeed where the other wise men
had failed? As the following verses show, the answer was a definitive yes.
Daniel answered the king, and said:

The secret which the king has demanded, the wise men, the astrologers, the
magicians, and the soothsayers cannot declare to the king. But there is a God
in heaven who reveals secrets, and He has made known to King
Nebuchadnezzar what will be in the latter days . . . . He who reveals secrets
has made known to you what will be. But as for me, this secret has not been
revealed to me because I have more wisdom than anyone living, but for our
sakes who make known the interpretation to the king, and that you may
know the thoughts of your heart (vv. 27–30).

This was not false humility. It was a sincere understanding of his role in
the event. To this youth, the issue was clear—it was about God, not Daniel.
And his actions revealed the trust he felt.

Application

Daniel would recite the dream and its interpretation accurately in verses 31–45,
but the key result is in verses 46–47—a declaration of the glory of Daniel's God.

In life, as with weather, there are times of high pressure and low pressure—but there are never times of no pressure. Our choices during these changing times tell a lot about us.

Where is our focus in times of pressure? Are we scrambling to protect ourselves at all costs? Are we doing desperate things that harm others in the process? Or are we more concerned about how our actions will reflect on our God?

In your thoughtful moments, ask God to showcase His presence in your life. Use these moments to line up with the eternal purposes and honor of God.

A Life of Confidence

To learn how to react with confidence during times of pressure and challenge.

MEMORY VERSE

Daniel 2:20—

"Blessed be the name of God forever and ever, for wisdom and might are His."

Warming Up

What situations cause you the most anxiety? What are your usual ways of coping with pressure-packed situations? What seems to work the best for you?

Thinking Through

1. When Daniel was approached to help with the problem of the uninterpreted dream, what high-pressure situation was he facing before he was even asked about the dream (p. 23; Daniel 2:13)?

2. Once Daniel was aware of the king's request, what did he and his friends do that Bill Crowder called "a powerful expression of their spiritual confidence"? What can we learn from this for our own pressure-packed times?

3. After God gave Daniel the dream information he needed, how did Daniel respond? What can we learn from that?

Going Further

Refer

1. How does 1 Corinthians 2:14 help us see that consulting God in prayer gives us an advantage over someone who does not do that?

2. In Daniel 2:27–30, Daniel deflected honor to God for this great feat. How does 1 Peter 5:5 apply here not only to Daniel but also to us?

1. Nebuchadnezzar consulted four groups (v. 2) for help in having his dream interpreted—perhaps those with the highest education and the best reputation for giving advice. Who might be a parallel group of people in today's world who are consulted for advice?

2. When the Chaldeans answered the king, they said, "There is not a man on earth who can tell the king's matter" (v. 10). Were they right? If so, then how was Daniel able to do what he did?

3. What was the full impact of Daniel's statement, "There is a God in heaven who reveals secrets" (v. 28) in a land like Babylon where various gods were worshiped?

¹ Now in the second year of Nebuchadnezzar's reign, [he] had dreams; and his spirit was so troubled that his sleep left him. ² Then the king gave the command to call the magicians, the astrologers, the sorcerers, and the Chaldeans to tell the king his dreams. . . . ¹⁰ The Chaldeans answered the king, and said, "There is not a man on earth who can tell the king's matter; . . . ¹² The king was angry and very furious, and gave the command to destroy all the wise men of Babylon . . . ¹⁶ So Daniel went in and asked the king to give him time, that he might tell the king the interpretation. ¹⁷ Then Daniel went to his house, and made the decision known to Hananiah, Mishael, and Azariah, his companions, ¹⁸ that they might seek mercies from the God of heaven . . . ¹⁹ Then the secret was revealed to Daniel in a night vision. . . . ²⁸ There is a God in heaven who reveals secrets, and He has made known to King Nebuchadnezzar what will be in the latter days.

Prayer Time ▶

Use the *Our Daily Bread* article on the next page as a guide for a devotional and meditation time relating to the culture.

Reflect

1. What can we learn about courage and faith from verse 16, which tells us that "Daniel went in and asked the king to give him time"?

2. The next time you are faced with a pressure-packed situation, how will Daniel's response here help you?

A Pattern for Prayer

Daniel had many wonderful traits. Evidently he was handsome, intelligent, and possessed outstanding abilities. He had deep convictions and great courage, and he dared to stand for the right—even though it would bring disfavor from the king. One of his finest characteristics was that he was a man of prayer! In Daniel 2 we find him calling his friends to pray in time of an extreme emergency. In chapter 6 we see him kneeling three times a day according to his custom; and in chapter 9 we hear him utter one of the most outstanding petitions of confession in the entire Word of God.

Note three facts concerning Daniel's prayer life. In Daniel 2:16 he is doing everything possible to answer his own requests! Aware of the crisis he and his friends are facing, he goes to the king himself, asking for more time. In verses 17 and 18 we see him calling for group prayer! He tells Shadrach, Meshach, and Abednego to begin praying with him that the God of heaven would reveal the king's dream. Then in verse 19, after Daniel's request has been granted, he is heard giving thanks and praise to the Lord for His gracious answers! Let us put these principles into practice in our own lives: First, do all we can to answer our own petitions; then, call for the prayers of others; and, finally, always remember to give thanks.

Be a twenty-first century Daniel: a *praying, working, thankful* believer!

—*Richard DeHaan*

DANIEL 2:17–18—Daniel went to his house, and made the decision known to . . . his companions, that they might seek mercies from the God of heaven.

■ Read today's *Our Daily Bread* at **www.rbc.org/odb**

4

A Life of Courage

DANIEL 5

O s Guinness writes in *The Call* that coming of age in the 1960s was "a bracing privilege." No one could take anything for granted. For thinking people, everything was challenged and taken back to square one. Guinness continues:

Nowhere was this more plain than in knowing what we believed and why. . . . And the ABC (or "anything but Christianity") mood of the decade often meant that any religion was fresh, relevant, and exciting as long as it was not Christian, orthodox, or traditional (p. 145).

A New King
(5:1–4)

As we approach Daniel 5, we see a man who challenged everything—especially the God Nebuchadnezzar had turned to years before (4:34–37). The year is 538 BC, twenty-three years after Nebuchadnezzar's death. The new king is Nebuchadnezzar's grandson Belshazzar—a man devoted to any god but the true God. It's a devotion that would bring his own downfall and that of his kingdom. The city of Babylon was under siege by the armies of the Medo-Persian empire. And Daniel, now between eighty and eighty-five years old, had to confront him.

Like Nero fiddling while Rome burned, Belshazzar ordered a national holiday—in spite of the siege that threatened the city.

> *Belshazzar the king made a great feast for a thousand of his lords, and drank wine in the presence of the thousand (v. 1).*

Why would he do that? Several reasons are possible. First, it was to put the people at ease. Like someone who nervously whistles his way through a graveyard, he invited a thousand city leaders to portray an atmosphere of confidence in spite of the danger. Second, Belshazzar may have wanted to show the authority of his kingdom. Third, he wanted to celebrate the Babylonian gods. These gods were displayed on the walls of the banquet hall, and Belshazzar led in toasting each of them in turn. When everyone was drunk, the king made his fatal mistake.

> *While he tasted the wine, Belshazzar gave the command to bring the gold and silver vessels which his father Nebuchadnezzar had taken from the temple which had been in Jerusalem, that the king and his lords, his wives, and his concubines might drink from them. Then they brought the gold vessels that had been taken from the temple of the house of God which had been in Jerusalem; and the king and his lords, his wives, and his concubines drank from them. They drank wine, and praised the gods of silver, bronze and iron, wood and stone (vv. 2–4).*

Remember, the kingdom is under siege and the king is trying to somehow prop up his shaky realm. So, in a drunken stupor, he calls for the temple vessels that were taken from Jerusalem years before. Why would he do this?

- Perhaps he wished to defy God.
- Perhaps he wanted to prove that the old prophecy (from Daniel to Belshazzar's grandfather) of Babylon's demise was false;
- Perhaps he remembered how Daniel had humbled Nebuchadnezzar and may have decided to show his superiority.

Whatever the reason, in a time when Belshazzar should have been fasting instead of feasting, he showed his utter contempt for the Most High God. He toasted his idols with vessels intended for the worship of God.

A New Challenge
(5:5–12)

God declared judgment with His handwriting on the wall—and the king saw it!

In the same hour the fingers of a man's hand appeared and wrote opposite the lampstand on the plaster of the wall of the king's palace; and the king saw the part of the hand that wrote. Then the king's countenance changed, and his thoughts troubled him, so that the joints of his hips were loosened and his knees knocked against each other. The king cried aloud to bring in the astrologers, the Chaldeans, and the soothsayers. The king spoke, saying to the wise men of Babylon, "Whoever reads this writing, and tells me its interpretation, shall be clothed with purple and have a chain of gold around his neck; and he shall be the third ruler in the kingdom" (vv. 5–7).

Belshazzar suddenly sobered up. He became pale and weak, and his knees knocked together. Earlier, he had been too drunk to stand. Now he was too frightened to!

He immediately offered a reward to anyone who could interpret the writing (v. 7). When all his wise men failed (v. 8), he "was greatly troubled, his countenance was changed, and his lords were astonished" (v. 9).

The king completely lost his cool because he faced a situation he couldn't control. The solution would come from an unlikely place.

The queen, because of the words of the king and his lords, came to the banquet hall. The queen spoke, saying "O king, live forever! Do not let your thoughts trouble you, nor let your countenance change. There is a man in your kingdom in whom is the Spirit of the Holy God. And in the days of your father, light and understanding and wisdom, like the wisdom of the gods, were found in him; and King Nebuchadnezzar your father—your father the king—made him chief of the magicians, astrologers, Chaldeans, and soothsayers. Inasmuch as an excellent spirit, knowledge, understanding, interpreting dreams, solving riddles, and explaining enigmas were found in this Daniel, whom the king named Belteshazzar, now let Daniel be called, and he will give the interpretation" (vv. 10–12).

A New Opportunity
(5:13–31)

Daniel, now an old man, arrived and was brought to the king (v. 13). What a scene! When Daniel saw the banquet hall with its idolatry, immorality, and defiance of God, imagine what was in the heart of this godly man who had sought to live a life of purity.

Belshazzar offered Daniel the reward for interpreting the dream, but Daniel would not be bought. The king said:

> *I have heard of you, that the Spirit of God is in you, and that light and understanding and excellent wisdom are found in you. Now the wise men, the astrologers, have been brought in before me, that they should read this writing and make known to me its interpretation, but they could not give the interpretation of the thing. And I have heard of you, that you can give interpretations and explain enigmas. Now if you can read the writing and make known to me its interpretation, you shall be clothed with purple and have a chain of gold around your neck, and shall be the third ruler in the kingdom (vv. 14–16).*

Notice that Daniel did not display the same level of compassion for this king that he had once shown to Nebuchadnezzar. He flatly refused the king's gifts and exposed his sin. Previously, he had counseled with compassion. But now he preached with fury.

Daniel told the king to keep his gifts. Then he proceeded to give him a history lesson. This history lesson went back to the days of Nebuchadnezzar (vv. 18–19) and once again brought to the surface the problem the king had with pride (vv. 20–21)—a problem shared by Belshazzar.

Before Daniel gave the interpretation, he declared God's judgment on Belshazzar and confirmed that his sin was not a sin of ignorance: "You . . . have not humbled your heart, although you knew all this" (v. 22). If not ignorance, what was it?

- It was arrogance (v. 23), seen in the king's defiant spirit.
- It was blasphemy (v. 23), displayed in the defiling of the temple vessels.
- It was idolatry (v. 23). Notice Daniel's sarcasm as he described the idols they were worshiping.
- It was rebellion (v. 23), because the king refused to let God be God.
- It deserved the judgment of God. The handwritten message on the wall indicated that judgment was coming (v. 24).

Belshazzar had failed to consider the power of the Most High God and His sovereign intervention.

The inscription on the wall is revealed in verse 25:

"MENE, MENE, TEKEL, UPHARSIN."

Daniel gave the interpretation of the message in verses 26–28:

This is the interprestaion of each word. MENE: God has numbered your kingdom, and finished it; TEKEL: You have been weighed in the balances, and found wanting; PERES: Your kingdom has been divided, and given to the Medes and the Persians.

Judgment was coming. How could it not? It was a classic case of Proverbs 29:1, "He who is often rebuked, and hardens his neck, will suddenly be destroyed, and that without remedy." There is no offer of relief or remedy; there was no way out, no loophole, no technicality—just the consequences of foolish choices.

Then Belshazzar gave the command, and they clothed Daniel with purple and put a chain of gold around his neck, and made a proclamation concerning him that he should be the third ruler in the kingdom. That very night Belshazzar, king of the Chaldeans, was slain. And Darius the Mede received the kingdom, being about sixty-two years old (vv. 29–31).

"That very night" it all happened. The seemingly impenetrable walls of Babylon were penetrated by the Medo-Persian armies and the city fell. The historian Xenophon tells us that Cyrus' general, Ugbaru, conquered Babylon by damming the river that flowed through the heart of the city. Then the army marched under the walls and conquered the city.

Notice, however, that before Belshazzar was killed and his kingdom conquered, he ordered the rewards to be given to Daniel, including that he be made the third highest ruler in the kingdom.

Application

Belshazzar, who was consumed by the same kind of pride that nearly destroyed his grandfather, tried to defy God. But he failed. The result was that he was "weighed in the balances and found wanting." This raises a key question that each of us needs to answer: How do I measure up?

How do I measure up—not in the eyes of the crowd but in the eyes of God, the Audience of One?

What we must never forget is that we are first and foremost called to live before the Audience of One—not other people. The issue before us is clear. May we so live that we measure up to God's design for our lives. To live, as Daniel did, to be measured only by the Lord.

A Life of Courage

MEMORY VERSE
Daniel 5:10–11 —

"O king, . . . there is a man in your kingdom in whom is the Spirit of the Holy God."

To see firsthand what can happen when a courageous person stands up for truth.

Warming Up

Was there ever a time when you had to stand up to someone in authority—knowing that he or she had the power but you had the truth? What happened?

Thinking Through

1. What is the situation in chapter 5 regarding the kings? What happened to Nebuchadnezzar, and what kind of person was this new king?

2. This time it wasn't a dream that needed interpretation (as in chapter 2). What was it? How did the king respond?

3. What were some of the problems with this king that Daniel pointed out before he interpreted the handwriting on the wall?

Going Further

Refer

1. In Revelation 17:5 and 18:2, John refers to ancient Babylon. What is the significance of that in relation to the context of those verses?

2. In Daniel 5:23, the prophet criticized Belshazzar for not giving God glory. See how important that is for us, according to 1 Corinthians 6:20.

1. From this story we get the idea, "the handwriting on the wall." What do people usually mean when they say this in modern society? Is today's meaning appropriate to apply to the situation at Belshazzar's feast?

2. When you read that the queen described Daniel as one "in whom is the Spirit of the Holy God" (v. 11), what stands out to you? How could it be possible today for someone to look at us and say the same thing?

3. In verse 17, Daniel made it clear before he interpreted the dream that he was not doing it for gifts. After the dream was interpreted, Belshazzar bestowed gifts on Daniel and he accepted them (v. 29). Why do you think he changed his mind?

¹ Belshazzar the king made a great feast for a thousand of his lords, ... ⁵ The fingers of a man's hand appeared and wrote opposite the lampstand on the plaster of the wall of the king's palace; and the king saw the part of the hand that wrote. . . . ¹⁰ The queen spoke, saying, "O king, live forever! Do not let your thoughts trouble you, nor let your countenance change. ¹¹ There is a man in your kingdom in whom is the Spirit of the Holy God. . . . ¹² now let Daniel be called, and he will give the interpretation.". . . . ²⁶ This is the interpretation of each word. MENE: God has numbered your kingdom, and finished it; ²⁷ TEKEL: You have been weighed in the balances, and found wanting; ²⁸ PERES: Your kingdom has been divided, and given to the Medes and Persians." ²⁹ Then Belshazzar gave the command, and they clothed Daniel with purple and put a chain of gold around his neck, and made a proclamation concerning him that he should be the third ruler in the kingdom.

Prayer Time ▶

Use the *Our Daily Bread* article on the next page as a guide for a devotional and meditation time relating to the culture.

Reflect

1. The key to Daniel's reputation—and the subsequent request for his help—resulted from his godliness (v. 11). What can we do to make sure we have that kind of reputation among those who know us?

2. How does Daniel's story in chapter 5 give you courage to be brave in the midst of trying circumstances?

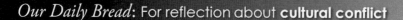

Courage To Stand Alone

It was a morally dark night in Babylon. Darker than your workplace, school, or community. King Belshazzar had willfully blasphemed God by desecrating the sacred goblets looted from the temple in Jerusalem. Now Babylon and Belshazzar were about to face God's judgment.

Yet in the midst of this gross darkness shone the light of a single witness: the prophet Daniel. Because of his reputation as a man with "the Spirit of the Holy God" (Daniel 5:11), Daniel was summoned to interpret the mystifying message on the wall.

Daniel could have softened God's warning to give it a meaning the king and his court would rather hear. He could have omitted the part about judgment and death. But instead of muddling the message to please the king, Daniel remained true to God. Standing alone before Belshazzar and his drunken court, he boldly spoke the whole truth.

It took enormous courage for Daniel to do that, but the threat from an earthly king was nothing compared to his allegiance to the King of heaven. Daniel feared Belshazzar so little because he feared God so much.

When we share Daniel's heavenly perspective, we find that God gives us the courage to stand alone too.

—*Haddon Robinson*

DANIEL 5:11—

There is a man in your kingdom in whom is the Spirit of the Holy God.

■ Read today's
Our Daily Bread at
www.rbc.org/odb

5

A Life of Devotion

DANIEL 6

W hat do we really need?" the TV commercial asks as you are swimming from the depths of the ocean to the surface. What do you need most? Shark repellent? Swim fins? Muscle power? The answer? What you need most is *oxygen*. It is the one thing you cannot survive without.

What is it that you cannot live without? Daniel will face that critical question next.

It is now about 538 BC, and Daniel, having spent almost his entire life in captivity, is an old man serving under his third ruler—Darius the Mede.

As chapter 6 opens, Darius has set up his government in Babylon. Daniel was made one of three governors over the entire realm (vv. 1–2). Everything in this new government was complex because of the weakness of a split kingdom (Cyrus of Persia; Darius of Media) and dual bureaucracies.

When Darius decided to elevate Daniel and put him in charge of the entire realm (v. 3), Daniel again found himself under scrutiny.

The Problem of Jealousy
(6:4–9)

So the governors and satraps sought to find some charge against Daniel concerning the kingdom; but they could find no charge or fault, because he was faithful; nor was there any error or fault found in him. Then these men said, "We shall not find any charge against Daniel unless we find it against him concerning the law of his God." So these governors and satraps thronged before the king, and said thus to him: "King Darius, live forever! All the governors of the kingdom, the administrators and satraps, the counselors and advisors, have consulted together to establish a royal statute and to make a firm decree, that whoever petitions any god or man for thirty days, except you, O king, shall be cast into the den of lions. Now, O king,

---

■ FOCAL POINT

"Daniel must have been over eighty years old at this time; these men had had many years to observe him. Yet there was nothing they could honestly accuse him of. So they resorted to a strategem. . . . Darius was trapped by this evil plot. He did not want to condemn Daniel, but he easily fell into this deception."

—James Montgomery Boice
Daniel: An Expositional Commentary

---

establish the decree and sign the writing, so that it cannot be changed, according to the law of the Medes and Persians, which does not alter."

These lower-level officials despised the fact that Daniel was in authority over them—and they wanted him removed. Pride is competitive, and envy is the result of wounded pride. C. S. Lewis wrote the following:

> Pride is essentially competitive. . . . Pride gets no pleasure out of having something, only out of having more of it than the next man. We say people are proud of being rich, or clever, or good-looking, but they are not. They are proud of being richer, or cleverer, or better-looking than others (*Mere Christianity*, p. 122).

These proud men were wounded by the elevation of a man of intergrity—and they wanted to destroy him for it.

How would they attack? They looked for grounds to accuse him, but they couldn't find any fault in him. Why? Because "he was faithful" (v. 4). This is quite a testimony—particularly coming from his enemies. In spite of living in an environment that was a moral cesspool, Daniel had stayed pure.

Attacking someone of impeccable character is a problem, so Daniel was attacked at his only perceivable point of weakness—his devotion to God. What a testimony! The only way to attack Daniel was to attack his relationship with God.

The officials conspired together and petitioned Darius with a united front (vv. 6–7), using deception to play on Darius' pride. They asked him to create a law that would make it illegal for the next thirty days to make a petition to any god or man—except to Darius himself. Since Darius was playing second fiddle to Cyrus the Persian, this decree elevated him to position of a god and enhanced the sense of the power that Cyrus had limited.

Notice the penalty for violating this decree: getting "cast into the den of lions" (v. 7). The jealousy of the officials knew no bounds. They wanted Daniel dead.

Darius affirmed their decree (v. 9), and since this was "the law of the Medes and the Persians," it couldn't be revoked. This explains why the decree was limited to thirty days. After Daniel was dead, they could get back to their normal lives.

Apparently, Darius was a good man. But, like all of us, he had weaknesses. In the heat of the moment, with his ego stroked, he made a rash decision and approved their law banning prayer.

 The Power of Testimony (6:10–11)

Daniel was so devoted to God that obedience to Him was more important than obedience to unjust laws. This illustrates the biblical principle of "obedient disobedience" in which we must choose between obeying God's Word or man. In the New Testament, we see this principle practiced by the apostles when they were commanded to stop preaching. They said, "We ought to obey God rather than men" (Acts 5:29).

Now when Daniel knew that the writing was signed, he went home. And in his upper room, with his windows open toward Jerusalem, he knelt down on his knees three times that day, and prayed and gave thanks before his God, as was his custom since early days (v. 10).

Daniel disobeyed the unjust law by praying. This is the secret of a pure life in the midst of an impure environment. He went about his regular business, unwilling to change or even appear to change to satisfy the crowd.

Then these men assembled and found Daniel praying and making supplication before his God (v. 11).

Daniel broke their law because it violated God's law—and he was caught. But the fear of being caught did not deter him. Daniel was willing to accept the consequences of being obedient to God. This is a hard but vital lesson. Keep in mind two things:

• We must be willing to accept the consequences for doing the right thing. The apostle Peter said, "But even if you should suffer for righteousness' sake, you are blessed" (1 Peter 3:14).

- God is still in control, even when life unfairly banishes us to the proverbial lions' den.

Daniel was caught praying to God, and he would suffer for righteousness' sake. But he was prepared to glorify God.

 The Peace of God
(6:12–17)

And they went before the king, and spoke concerning the king's decree: "Have you not signed a decree that every man who petitions any god or man within thirty days, except you, O king, shall be cast into the den of lions?" The king answered and said, "The thing is true, according to the law of the Medes and Persians, which does not alter." So they answered and said before the king, "That Daniel, who is one of the captives from Judah, does not show due regard for you, O king, or for the decree that you have signed, but makes his petition three times a day"
(vv. 12–13).

These men were certainly sly. First, they reminded Darius of his irrevocable decree. Then they leveled their attack with an accusation that was a mix of truth and slander. Daniel had not disregarded the king, but he did refuse to disregard his God.

And the king, when he heard these words, was greatly displeased with himself, and set his heart on Daniel to deliver him; and he labored till the going down of the sun to deliver him. Then these men approached the king, and said to the king, "Know, O king, that it is the law of the Medes and the Persians that no decree or statute which the king establishes may be changed"
(vv. 14–15).

Darius' response shows that he finally understood what was going on, for he was "greatly displeased with himself." He had exercised poor judgment and was grieved. It seems he was not displeased with Daniel or with Daniel's behavior but with his own pride.

Darius pursued Daniel's release because he didn't want him to suffer the consequences of the foolish decree (v. 14). He looked for a legal loophole, but there was none. He saw the impact of his actions and realized that he was too late. In effect, Darius was trapped by his own law (v. 15). There was no way out—Daniel had to be executed.

> *So the king gave the command, and they brought Daniel and cast him into the den of lions. But the king spoke, saying to Daniel, "Your God, whom you serve continually, He will deliver you." Then a stone was brought and laid on the mouth of the den, and the king sealed it with his own signet ring and with the signets of his lords, that the purpose concerning Daniel might not be changed (vv. 16–17).*

Having been found guilty of the crime of serving God continually (v. 16), Daniel was cast into the lions' den. These lions were there for the purpose of torturing prisoners. They were usually starved, mistreated, and taunted so they would rip a man to pieces.

In desperation, Darius tried to offer consolation to Daniel at his execution (v. 16). The den was then covered with a stone and sealed (v. 17).

Have you ever wondered what happened inside the lions' den once the stone was sealed? One Bible scholar suggests that Daniel slid to the cave floor and was approached by lions—only to have them lie around him to give him warmth and comfort for the cold night ahead!

 # The Protection of God
(6:18–23)

As Daniel slept peacefully with the lions, Darius had a very different kind of night. This highlights the difference between a clear conscience (Daniel's) and a heart full of guilt (Darius').

> *Now the king went to his palace and spent the night fasting; and no musicians were brought before him. Also his sleep went from him (v. 18).*

Worry, guilt, loss of sleep, loss of appetite—all were the effects of Darius' failure to discern the evil conspiracy of his officials. So, the king rose and went to the den of lions.

> *When he came to the den, he cried out with a lamenting voice to Daniel. The king spoke, saying to Daniel, "Daniel, servant of the living God, has your God, whom you serve continually, been able to deliver you from the lions?" Then Daniel said to the king, "O king, live forever! My God sent His angel and shut the lions' mouths, so that they have not hurt me, because I was found innocent before Him; and also, O king, I have done no wrong before you." Now the king was exceedingly glad for him, and commanded that they should take Daniel up out of the den. So Daniel was taken up out of the den, and no injury whatever was found on him, because he believed in his God (vv. 20–23).*

After a sleepless night, Darius went to see what had happened. He was almost pathetic as he called into the den that should hold no human life. Even in the words of Darius, we see the profound impact of Daniel's life on him: "Has your God, whom you serve continually, been able to deliver you from the lions?" It's amazing that Darius even considered the possibility that God protected Daniel from the lions. Then, from out of the darkness, came Daniel's calm, confident reply that God, in fact, had protected him.

Daniel was not hurt, "because he believed in his God" (6:23). Hebrews 11:33 also tells us that it was Daniel's faith that "stopped the mouth of lions." Of course, as Hebrews 11:35–40 indicates, it's not always God's will to deliver His children. In the early church, untold thousands of martyrs were fed to lions and ushered into eternity. But whether or not God delivers at any particular moment, His ability to deliver is never diminished. He is always able.

5 A Life of Devotion

MEMORY VERSE

Daniel 6:10—

"When Daniel knew that the writing was signed, he . . . knelt down on his knees three times that day, and prayed . . . as was his custom."

To understand the importance of remaining faithful in worship and prayer, no matter what the obstacles might be.

Warming Up

What are some devotional habits that have helped you and that you can share with others? Is there a resource or prayer routine that helps you?

Thinking Through

1. Bill Crowder, in explaining the feelings the lower-level officials had toward Daniel, said this: "Pride is competitive, and envy is the result of wounded pride" (p. 43). How have you seen that lived out in lives around you?

2. Daniel was attacked, verse 4 says, because "he was faithful." Have you seen that reality in your life or in the lives of other Christians you know? How would it feel to do the right thing before God but be attacked by men?

3. Bill Crowder said, "Daniel disobeyed the unjust law" (p. 44). Is that something you've ever had to do? If not, what do you see on the horizon that might be a law you would have to disobey if it clashed with God's Word?

Going Further

Refer

1. Daniel was a man of strong faith. Examine Hebrews 11:6 and see how Daniel's life mirrors that verse. How can it relate to us as Christians attempting to manifest faith in our lives?

2. Read James 2:14–20 and see what elements of faith can be found in that passage.

1. Contemplate and discuss the significance of verse 4 regarding Daniel. What would it mean in our community if these things could be said of us?

2. In verse 10, Daniel committed an act of defiance toward a given law. How does that square with Romans 13:1–2?

3. What does Daniel's response in verse 21 tell us about his character?

⁴ The governors and satraps sought to find some charge against Daniel concerning the kingdom; but they could find no charge or fault, because he was faithful; nor was there any error or fault found in him. . . . ⁷ [They] consulted together to establish a royal statute . . . that whoever petitions any god or man for thirty days, except you, O king, shall be cast into the den of lions. . . . ¹⁰ Daniel knew that the writing was signed, . . . And in his upper room, with his windows open toward Jerusalem, he knelt down on his knees three times that day, and prayed and gave thanks before his God, . . . ¹⁶ They brought Daniel and cast him into the den of lions. . . . ²⁰ When [the king] came to the den, he cried out with a lamenting voice to Daniel. . . . ²¹ Then Daniel said to the king, "O king, live forever!" ²² My God sent His angel and shut the lions' mouths, so that they have not hurt me, because I was found innocent before Him; and also, O king, I have done no wrong before you."

Prayer Time ⫸

Use the *Our Daily Bread* article on the next page as a guide for a devotional and meditation time relating to the culture.

Reflect

1. How can Daniel's example spur us on to greater prayerfulness? What are two or three actual changes that this story can suggest for our prayer lives?

2. In Daniel 6:4 and 6:22, Daniel's life seems pretty much flawless, and we don't stack up. How can we emulate him even though we may not match his seeming flawlessness?

Looking for Success?

Success comes in various forms, but for the believer, it is achieved only through doing God's will.

John W. Yates was so poor that he had to put cardboard in his shoes to cover up the holes. When he opened a bank account at the age of fifteen, he deposited the little earnings he had under the name "John W. Yates and Company." You see, from his youth he made God his partner and manager, and he carried that practice into his business. In time, he became a multimillionaire.

Another young man, Oswald Chambers of Scotland, showed much artistic promise. At eighteen he was invited to study under Europe's greatest masters. But he declined and enrolled in a Bible school, where he eventually became a teacher. Later, he went to Egypt and ministered to the spiritual needs of British soldiers. Chambers died there in his forties, but he left to the world a rich legacy of devotional literature. Both men made doing God's will their prime objective; both were a success.

Daniel began his career as a young captive in Babylon. Repeatedly he put his life on the line to remain faithful to the Lord. He refused to compromise, and God elevated him to a position of prominence. When we take that kind of attitude and accept whatever God has for us, we can be sure of success, no matter what form it takes.

—*Herb Vander Lugt*

DANIEL 6:28—

Daniel prospered in the reign of Darius and in the reign of Cyrus the Persian.

■ Read today's
Our Daily Bread at
www.rbc.org/odb

6

Making a Decision

When we read the story of Daniel and how he handled his difficult circumstances more than two thousand years after it happened, we know the outcome.

But Daniel didn't.

He knew God's ability, but he didn't know all the details of God's plan. He only knew that he wanted to live in a way that would honor God. That meant making a decision to obey God rather than submit to the most powerful government of his day.

Daniel also knew that he couldn't survive without expressing his heart to God. It's been said that God's Word is the milk, meat, and bread of life. But prayer is its breath. You can live for a long period of time without food, but you can't survive more than a few minutes without breath. That's how important prayer is. But do we give prayer that kind of priority in our lives? This is the essence of spiritual living in the midst of a secular culture.

 The Need of the Hour

Preacher E. M. Bounds wrote, "The church is looking for better methods; God is looking for better men" (*Power Through Prayer*, p. 9).

The unfolding drama of Daniel shouts that same message to us. We are living in a Babylonian-like world. We are surrounded by an ever-changing, constantly deteriorating culture. Yet, it is to this kind of world that we are called to be the Daniels of our own generation. We can either be poured into the mold of our culture, or like Daniel, we can use the darkness as an opportunity to reflect the light of our God.

The choice is ours.

How will we, as men and women of God, serve God in our generation? We can start by emulating Daniel's gracious courage to live his life to honor God—which is a wonderful example and legacy for us.

It is possible, however, that you have not yet begun to live in the spirit of Daniel's God. If not, you can meet the Savior in the pages of the New Testament.

According to the Gospel writers, Daniel's God came to us in the person of His Son Jesus Christ. After three years of public life, Jesus voluntarily died on an executioner's cross to pay for our sins.

Three days later He rose from the dead.

Now He offers the free gift of forgiveness to all who will acknowledge their hopeless condition and trust Him and His gift. If you believe in this Christ but have never personally opened your heart to Him, then claim the promise of the apostle John, who wrote the following:

As many as received Him, to them He gave the right to become children of God, to those who believe in His name (John 1:12).

By trusting Jesus as your Savior, you not only have your sins forgiven and have the promise of an eternal home in heaven, but you also have the power and the resources Daniel had in his relationship with God. You can move forward with courage—even in a world and a culture that stands opposed to God and His goodness.

6 Making a Decision

MEMORY VERSE
John 1:12 —

"As many as received Him, to them He gave the right to become children of God, to those who believe in His name."

To ensure we have established a relationship with God so that we have the basis of faith that supports all who want to live for Him.

Warming Up

What is your "testimony," or your story of faith? Would it be helpful to share your story with the others in your group?

Thinking Through

1. Bill Crowder says that Daniel knew what God could do, "but he didn't know all the details of God's plan" (p. 51). That is the essence of faith—trusting God with the unknown (see Hebrews 11:1). How has that played out in your life?

2. The starting point for all of us in our attempt to be a Daniel in our world is to accept "the free gift of forgiveness" (p. 52). Why is that so very important for every person?

3. John 1:12 says we can become "children of God." Some say we are all God's children. What is the distinction that is being suggested with this verse?

Going Further

Refer

1. Examine the meaning in the following passages: John 3:16; Ephesians 2:8–9; Romans 3:23; Romans 5:8; Romans 6:23.

1. If we take the term *Word* here to mean "Jesus," what do verses 1 and 2 tell us about God and Jesus?

2. Who is the "Light" John came to bear witness about? How does the Light give us light? (v. 9)

3. What does it mean to "believe in His [Jesus'] name" (v. 12)? What did He do that should cause us to trust Him? Have you been "born . . . of God" (v. 13)?

¹ In the beginning was the Word, and the Word was with God, and the Word was God. ² He was in the beginning with God. ³ All things were made through Him, and without Him nothing was made that was made. ⁴ In Him was life, and the life was the light of men. . . . ⁶ There was a man sent from God, whose name was John. ⁷ This man came for a witness, to bear witness of the Light, that all through him might believe. ⁸ He was not that Light, but was sent to bear witness of that Light. ⁹ That was the true Light which gives light to every man coming into the world. ¹⁰ He was in the world, and the world was made through Him, and the world did not know Him. ¹¹ He came to His own, and His own did not receive Him. ¹² But as many as received Him, to them He gave the right to become children of God, to those who believe in His name: ¹³ who were born, not of blood, nor of the will of the flesh, nor of the will of man, but of God.

Prayer Time ⟩

Use the *Our Daily Bread* article on the next page as a guide for a devotional and meditation time relating to the culture.

Reflect

1. To live by faith as Daniel did would be an awesome thing. What are some lessons from Daniel's life that can help me do that?

2. Have I responded to the "Need of the Hour" (p. 52)?

Steps To Nowhere

As finite creatures, we sense that our earthly life and eternal destiny are somehow bound up with our Creator. Most religions represent man's effort to reach up to God and become acceptable to Him. In China, for example, devout pilgrims ascend a sacred mountain called Taishan. They climb seven thousand steps to its summit, first passing through the "middle gate," then through "heaven's southern gate." Finally they reach a beautiful building—the Temple of the Azure Cloud. Here they offer sacrifices, thinking they'll gain God's favor. Such effort represents great religious fervor, but it brings the devotee no closer to God.

By contrast, Christianity begins with the Creator of heaven and earth reaching down to man. In His holiness He is beyond the highest mountain peak, so far out of reach of sinful man that only He himself could span the gulf. And that's exactly what He did. By the miracle of the incarnation, He became flesh and offered himself a sacrifice for man's sin. Then, after rising from the dead, He went back to Glory. This descent-ascent, with its accompanying eternal sacrifice, was for us. Our part is to confess our sin, renounce all efforts to earn our salvation, and trust Him as our Savior.

Are you still climbing endless steps of self-effort that lead nowhere? Why not take that one all-important step of faith in Jesus? It's the step that leads to heaven.

—*Dennis DeHaan*

JOHN 1:12—

As many as received Him, to them He gave the right to become children of God, to those who believe in His name.

■ Read today's *Our Daily Bread* at **www.rbc.org/odb**

■ LEADER'S and USER'S GUIDE

Overview of Lessons

Pulpit Sermon Series (for pastors and church leaders)

Although the Discovery Series Bible Study is primarily for personal and group study, pastors may want to use this material as the foundation for a series of messages on this important issue. The suggested topics and their corresponding texts from the Overview of Lessons above can be used as an outline for a sermon series.

DSBS User's Guide (for individuals and small groups)

Individuals—Personal Study

• Read the designated pages of the book.

• Carefully consider the study questions, and write out answers for each.

Small Groups—Bible-Study Discussion

• To maximize the value of the time spent together, each member should do the lesson work prior to the group meeting.

• Recommended discussion time: 45 minutes.

• Engage the group in a discussion of the questions—seeking full participation from each member.

Note To The Reader

The publisher invites you to share your response to the message of this book by writing Discovery House Publishers, P.O. Box 3566, Grand Rapids, MI 49501, USA. For information about other Discovery House books, music, videos, or DVDs, contact us at the same address or call 1–800–653–8333. Find us on the Internet at **http://www.dhp.org/** or send e-mail to **books@dhp.org**.